AF507155

This book belongs to
Ocean Cruiser

To every student I've had the opportunity to impact,
thank you.

-Signed, Mr. Moultrie

ISBN 9798338256749

It was a bright Saturday morning, and the sun peeked cheerfully
through the curtains of Alex and Gabbie's room.

The air was filled with the sounds of their favorite cartoons, but today, the magic of the television could hardly compare to the adventure that awaited them. As they munched on their breakfast cereal, the room seemed to hum with the promise of an extraordinary day ahead.

Suddenly, Alex's eyes gleamed with an idea. "Gabbie, let's build a submarine today!" he exclaimed, jumping up so fast his cereal spoon clattered to the floor. Gabbie's face lit up with excitement, and they both scrambled to gather their materials.

Pillows became the sturdy base, blankets draped over chairs transformed into a shimmering hull, and their old cardboard box, decorated with markers and stickers, turned into a control panel filled with mysterious buttons and levers.

With a countdown fit for a grand launch, Alex and Gabble shouted, "Three, two, one, blast off!" Their living room, now a command center for their underwater voyage, was ready to take them to the unknown depths of the ocean.

The walls of their fort seemed to pulse with the energy of the deep sea as they crawled inside, their imaginations already swimming with the creatures they might meet. The adventure was just beginning, and their hearts raced with anticipation.

As the makeshift periscope (a rolled-up piece of shiny wrapping paper) showed the first glimpses of the colorful coral reefs, Alex and Gabbie gasped in awe.

The submarine dived deeper, and the vibrant coral came alive with bustling fish darting in and out. "Look, Gabbie!" Alex pointed excitedly at a clownfish peeking from behind a coral fan.

As they ventured further, the busy coral gave way to the open ocean. Here, dolphins leaped joyfully around their submarine, their clicks and songs filling the sea. Far below, the shadowy figures of whales gilded silently by.

The sunlight faded as they descended into the mysterious deep sea. Here, strange creatures like the glowing anglerfish guided their path. Gabbie gasped as a giant squid flashed by, its tentacles almost brushing their submarine.

Nearing the ocean floor, the submarine sailed over lush seagrass meadows. Tiny seahorses gripped the waving seaweed, and curious crabs scuttled underneath, peeking out from their hiding spots to watch the siblings pass.

The water cooled as they reached the Arctic waters. Icebergs loomed large above, and playful penguins slid down their icy sides. Beneath the waves, seals frolicked, their thick fur protecting them from the chill.

With a whoosh, their submarine surfaced. As the living room returned to normal, Alex and Gabbie laughed, filled with joy from their ocean adventure.

"What will we explore next?" Alex pondered, eyes twinkling. "Maybe Outer Space!" Gabbie exclaimed, already dreaming of their next adventure.

Learn About The Ocean

Penguin: A type of bird that can't fly but is an excellent swimmer
Submarine: A type of ship that can travel underwater.
Coral Reef: A colorful underwater structure made of coral, home to many sea creatures.
Dolphin: A smart sea animal known for its playful behavior.
Whale: The largest mammal that lives in the ocean.
Fish: A creature that lives in water, has gills, and swims with fins.
Squid: A sea animal with eight arms and a soft body.
Seahorse: A small fish that swims upright and has a horse-like head.
Anglerfish: A fish that lives deep in the ocean and has a glowing light to attract prey.

Think About The Ocean

Recall Questions:
What did Alex and Gabbie use to explore the ocean?
Name three animals that Alex and Gabbie saw in the ocean.
What happened when Alex and Gabbie followed the glowing anglerfish?

Critical Thinking Questions:
Why do you think Alex and Gabbie saw different animals at the bottom of the ocean than near the coral reef?
How do you think the submarine helps Alex and Gabbie stay safe underwater?

Additional Activities:
Encourage students to draw their own underwater scene, including their favorite ocean animals. They can imagine they are Alex or Gabbie and illustrate what they might see on their adventure.

About The Author

Johnnie D. Moultrie is an accomplished educator and author with a passion for inspiring young minds. With years of experience in education, he has successfully guided countless students, fostering a love for learning and creativity. As the author of several successful books, Johnnie continues to share his gift for storytelling, captivating young readers with the magic of imagination. Join him on his journey through this enchanting series, where he brings the wonders of the world to life through the eyes of curious and adventurous children.

A Letter To My Students

To all my beloved students, my cherished nieces and nephews,

As I reflect on the years we've spent together in the classroom and beyond, my heart is filled with immense gratitude. Thank you for welcoming me not just as your teacher, but as a part of your villages. Your acceptance allowed me to be my truest self, to teach with passion, and to learn from each of you in return. The bonds we've formed and the trust you've placed in me are treasures I carry with me into this new chapter. Each of you has enriched my life, teaching me as much, if not more, than I could have ever taught you. You've shown me the power of connection, the strength of community, and the enduring impact of genuine relationships. As we continue to grow and navigate new paths, remember that our journey together has been a profound part of my story, and I hope it has positively shaped yours too. Let's keep striving, keep supporting one another, and always remain connected.

With all my appreciation and love,

Mr. Johnnie D. Moultrie aka Mr. Moultrie

Check Out the Series

Join Alex & Gabbie in all of their thrills and adventures! Check out the other storybooks and activity books!

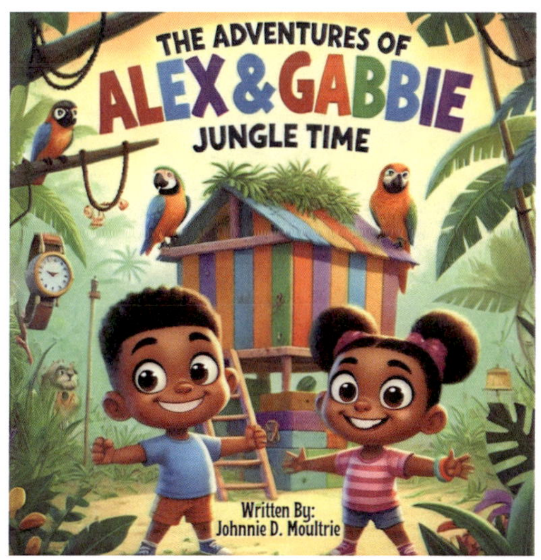